RED

By Patricia M. Stockland
Illustrated by Julia Woolf

Content Consultant
Susan Kesselring, MA
Literacy Educator and Preschool Director

STOP

magic
wagon

(COLORS)

visit us at www.abdopublishing.com

Published by Magic Wagon, a division of the ABDO Publishing Group, 8000 West 78th Street, Edina, Minnesota 55439. Copyright © 2009 by Abdo Consulting Group, Inc. International copyrights reserved in all countries. All rights reserved. No part of this book may be reproduced in any form without written permission from the publisher.

Looking Glass Library™ is a trademark and logo of Magic Wagon.

Printed in the United States.

Text by Patricia M. Stockland
Illustrations by Julia Woolf
Edited by Jill Sherman
Interior layout and design by Nicole Brecke
Cover Design by Nicole Brecke

Library of Congress Cataloging-in-Publication Data

Stockland, Patricia M.
  Red / by Patricia M. Stockland ; illustrated by Julia Woolf.
     p. cm. — (Colors)
  ISBN 978-1-60270-258-5
  1. Red—Juvenile literature. 2. Color—Juvenile literature. I. Woolf, Julia, ill. II. Title.
  QC495.5.S774 2009
  535.6—dc22
                          2008001625

Mom and I get into the car.

The car is red.

4

Mom stops at the stoplight.

The stoplight is red.

Mom stops at the stop sign.

The stop sign is red.

8

Mom and I walk to the big barn.

The barn is red.

We ride in an old wagon.

The wagon is red.

11

12

We pick big apples.

The apples are red.

Mom buys me a balloon.

The balloon is red.

15

16

I see a bright bird.

The bird is red.

We smell a sweet rose.

The rose is red.

19

20

Mom gives me a kiss.

The kiss is red!

What Is Red?

There are three primary colors: red, blue, and yellow. These colors combine to create other colors. You cannot make the color red by mixing other colors. You can make red darker or lighter by adding black or white.

Primary Colors

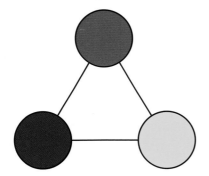 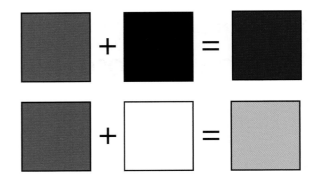

Some colors seem cool. Others seem warm. What colors remind you of a warm fire? What about a cool lake? What red things did you see in the story? Does red seem warm or cool to you? Red is a warm color!

Words to Know

bright—having a lot of color; a bright object stands out and can be seen easily.

rose—a sweet-smelling flower.

smell—to get the scent of something using your nose.

wagon—a cart with four wheels that is pulled by horses or a tractor.

Web Sites

To learn more about the color red, visit ABDO Publishing Company on the World Wide Web at **www.abdopublishing.com**. Web sites about the colors are featured on our Book Links page. These links are routinely monitored and updated to provide the most current information available.